States

MICHIGAN

by Jordan Mills

CAPSTONE PRESS
a capstone imprint

Next Page Books are published by Capstone Press,
1710 Roe Crest Drive, North Mankato, Minnesota 56003
www.mycapstone.com

Library of Congress Cataloging-in-Publication Data
Cataloging-in-publication information is on file with the Library of
Congress.
ISBN 978-1-5157-0409-6 (library binding)
ISBN 978-1-5157-0468-3 (paperback)
ISBN 978-1-5157-0520-8 (ebook PDF)

Editorial Credits
Jaclyn Jaycox, editor; Richard Korab and Katy LaVigne, designers;
Morgan Walters, media researcher; Laura Manthe, production specialist

Photo Credits
Alamy: Chronicle, 26, Everett Collection Historical, 27; AP Images:
Kellog Co., bottom 18; Capstone Press: Angie Gahler, map 4, 7;
CriaImages.com: Jay Robert Nash Collection, middle 18; Getty Images:
PhotoQuest, 28, Time & Life Pictuers/James Keyser, middle 19, Visuals
Unlimited, Inc./Jana Jirak, bottom left 21; iStockphoto: lemonadelucy,
top right 21; Library of Congress: Prints and Photographs Division, top
19; North Wind Picture Archives, 12; One Mile Up, Inc., flag, seal 23;
Shutterstock: Aivoges, 29, artcphotos, 16, Benjamin Simeneta, 10, Chris
Hill, bottom left 20, Colin D. Young, bottom right 21, ehrlif, 7, Ffooter,
13, istetiana, top 24, Jason Patrick Ross, top left 21, Jeff Feverston,
bottom right 20, John McCormick, 5, bottom left 8, kanusommer,
top right 20, Katherine Welles, bottom 24, Ken Wolter, top left 20,
LunaseeStudios, 15, Maleo, 14, Mark Baldwin, 11, Michael G Smith, 9,
Rena Schild, bottom 19, Rudy Balasko, cover, s_bukley, top 18, Sergey
Kohl, 25, Shriram Patki, bottom right 8, Susan Montgomery, 17, Tom
Reichner, middle left 21, Vince Ruffa, 6

All design elements by Shutterstock

Printed and bound in the United States.
PO_836

TABLE OF CONTENTS

Want to take your research further? Ask your librarian if your school subscribes to PebbleGo Next. If so, when you see this helpful symbol ⟨↖⟩ throughout the book, log onto www.pebblegonext.com for bonus downloads and information.

LOCATION

Michigan is in the northern United States. Michigan is made up of the Upper and Lower Peninsulas. The state is surrounded by four of the five Great Lakes. Lake Michigan borders the Lower Peninsula to the west. Lake Huron lies to the east, and Lake Superior is to the north. Lake Erie borders a small part of southeastern Michigan. Indiana and Ohio form the land border to the south. Wisconsin borders the Upper Peninsula to the southwest. Detroit, the state's largest city, lies north of part of the province of Ontario, Canada. Ontario also borders Michigan to the north at Sault Sainte Marie.

Michigan's next two largest cities are Grand Rapids and Warren. The capital, Lansing, is near the middle of the Lower Peninsula.

PebbleGo Next Bonus!
To print and label your own map, go to www.pebblegonext.com and search keywords:

MI MAP

The Great Lakes make up the largest body of freshwater on Earth.

GEOGRAPHY

Michigan is almost completely surrounded by water. Michigan also has more than 11,000 lakes. Farms, large cities, and low rolling hills fill the southern part of the Lower Peninsula. Forests cover much of the northern Lower Peninsula. The Upper Peninsula is known for its wooded mountains and waterfalls. The land is rugged in the west and swampy in the east. Mount Arvon, the state's highest point at 1,980 feet (604 meters) above sea level, is in the western part of the region. Mackinac Island sits between Michigan's two peninsulas.

PebbleGo Next Bonus! To watch a video about Michigan's auto industry, go to www.pebblegonext.com and search keywords:

MI VIDEO

Mackinac Island is located on Lake Huron.

Ludington State Park lies between Hamlin Lake and Lake Michigan.

Legend

▲ Highest Point

◯ Lake

◯ Point of Interest

〰 River

Isle Royale National Park

Lake Superior

▲ Mount Arvon

Straits of Mackinac

UPPER PENINSULA

Mackinac Island

Menominee River

Lake Huron

Sleeping Bear Dunes National Lakeshore

Houghton Lake

Lake Michigan

LOWER PENINSULA

Lake St. Clair

Lake Erie

Scale

Miles

0   25   50   75   100

0   25   50   75   100   125   150

Kilometers

WEATHER

Michigan has cold winters and mild summers. Michigan's average winter temperature is 22 degrees Fahrenheit (minus 6 degrees Celsius). Its average summer temperature is 66°F (19°C).

Average High and Low Temperatures (Lansing, MI)

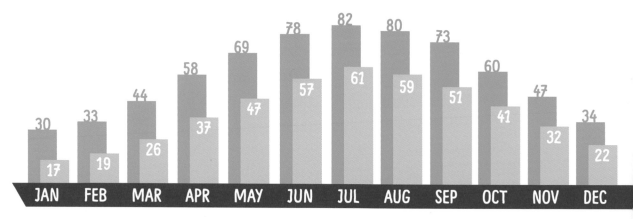

	JAN	FEB	MAR	APR	MAY	JUN	JUL	AUG	SEP	OCT	NOV	DEC
High	30	33	44	58	69	78	82	80	73	60	47	34
Low	17	19	26	37	47	57	61	59	51	41	32	22

Mackinac Island

Mackinac Island sits between Michigan's two peninsulas. Cars are not allowed on the island. Most people ride bicycles. Some people also ride horses. Mackinac Island is famous for its rocky shoreline, hiking trails, and its fudge. Several shops on the island sell homemade fudge.

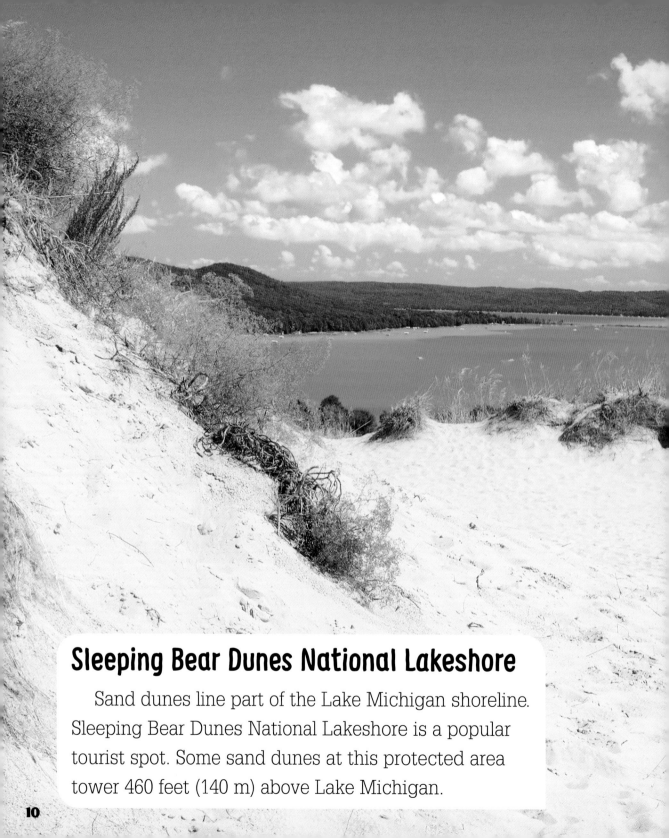

Sleeping Bear Dunes National Lakeshore

Sand dunes line part of the Lake Michigan shoreline. Sleeping Bear Dunes National Lakeshore is a popular tourist spot. Some sand dunes at this protected area tower 460 feet (140 m) above Lake Michigan.

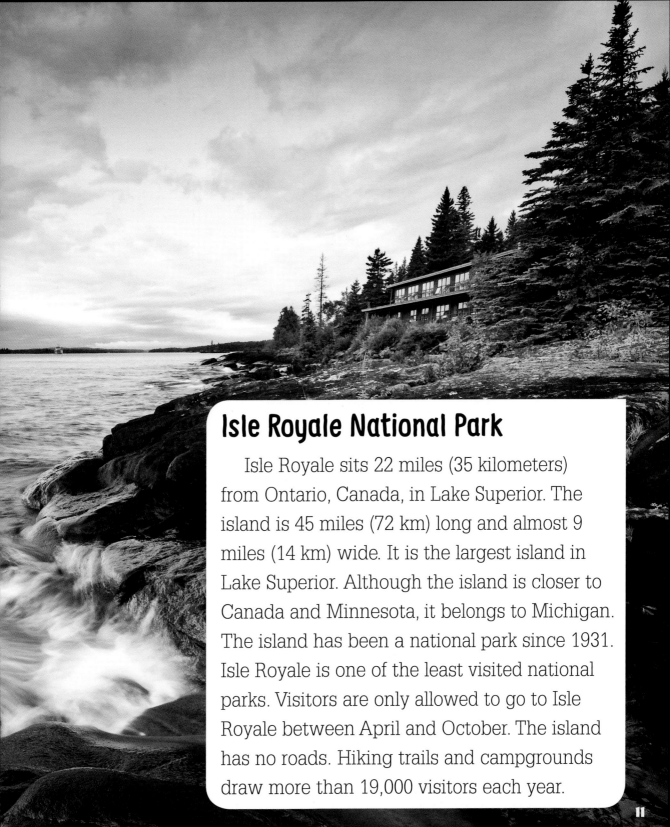

Isle Royale National Park

Isle Royale sits 22 miles (35 kilometers) from Ontario, Canada, in Lake Superior. The island is 45 miles (72 km) long and almost 9 miles (14 km) wide. It is the largest island in Lake Superior. Although the island is closer to Canada and Minnesota, it belongs to Michigan. The island has been a national park since 1931. Isle Royale is one of the least visited national parks. Visitors are only allowed to go to Isle Royale between April and October. The island has no roads. Hiking trails and campgrounds draw more than 19,000 visitors each year.

HISTORY AND GOVERNMENT

The Sault Sainte Marie Canal connects Lake Superior and Lake Huron.

In 1688 French priest Jacques Marquette started the first European settlement in Michigan. The settlement, Sault Sainte Marie, was located in the eastern part of the Upper Peninsula. The French built other forts throughout Michigan to protect their fur trade from the British. The British and French fought the French and Indian wars (1689–1763). American Indians helped the French. When the wars ended, the British took over the French forts. When the American colonists won the Revolutionary War (1775–1783), Michigan became part of the U.S. Northwest Territory. In 1837 Michigan became the 26th state.

Michigan's state government is divided into three branches. The legislative branch makes the state's laws and includes the 38-member Senate and 110-member House of Representatives. The executive branch makes sure the laws are carried out. Michigan's governor heads the executive branch. Michigan's judges and courts make up the judicial branch. They uphold the laws.

Michigan's state capitol building is located in Lansing.

INDUSTRY

Michigan is a major manufacturing state. Michigan produces more cars and trucks than any other state. Companies in Michigan also produce chemicals and medicines. People do medical research at the state's colleges. Food manufacturing companies in Battle Creek produce more breakfast cereal than any other city in the world. The headquarters for the Kellogg Company is in Battle Creek.

Grain and corn farmers take advantage of the long growing season in the southern

Michigan ranks fourth in the nation for producing sweet cherries.

part of the Lower Peninsula. Orchards can be found along the Lake Michigan shoreline. Cherries, plums, peaches, and grapes are the main fruit crops. Michigan grapes are made into juice and wine. Michigan grows more tart cherries than any other state.

Michigan's natural resources are important to the state's economy. Tourism and the furniture and paper industries all depend on Michigan's forests. Mines in the Upper Peninsula produce iron ore.

Kellogg's makes popular cereals like Corn Flakes.

POPULATION

Most people in Michigan have European backgrounds. Many Polish people moved to Michigan in the early 1900s to work in Henry Ford's automobile factory. About 120,000 Dutch people settled around Grand Rapids and Holland in the mid-1800s. Many other Michiganians have German ancestors. In the Upper Peninsula, the largest ethnic group comes from Finland.

Michigan was an important part of the Underground Railroad in the 1800s. Many African-Americans chose to settle in Michigan. African-Americans now make up about 14 percent of Michigan's population.

Population by Ethnicity

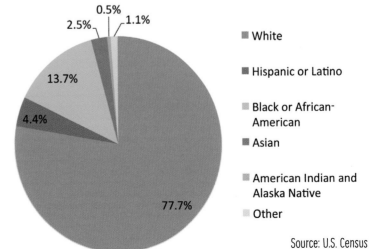

0.5%
2.5%
1.1%
13.7%
4.4%
77.7%

- White
- Hispanic or Latino
- Black or African-American
- Asian
- American Indian and Alaska Native
- Other

Source: U.S. Census Bureau

The next largest ethnic group in Michigan is Hispanics, who make up more than 4 percent of the population. Asians make up more than 2 percent of the population.

FAMOUS PEOPLE

Earvin "Magic" Johnson (1959–) is from Lansing. He was one of the best basketball players of all time. In his time with the Los Angeles Lakers, Johnson won five NBA championships and was league Most Valuable Player three times.

Henry Ford (1863–1947) founded the Ford Motor Company in Detroit. His Model T Ford was very popular. He raised his workers' minimum wage to $5 a day — more than twice the usual rate at that time.

William Kellogg (1860–1951) invented cornflakes. He founded the Kellogg's breakfast cereal company in Battle Creek.

Gerald R. Ford Jr. (1913–2006) was the 38th president of the United States (1974–1977). He was the vice president under Richard Nixon and became president in 1974 when Nixon resigned. He was born in Nebraska and grew up in Grand Rapids.

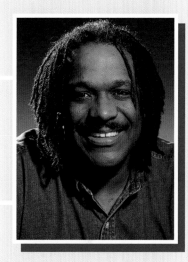

Christopher Paul Curtis (1953–) is a children's book author. His book *Bud, Not Buddy* won the Newbery Award in 2000. He was born and raised in Flint.

Derek Jeter (1974–) was a pro baseball star for the New York Yankees. He helped his team win the World Series five times during his long career. He grew up in Kalamazoo.

STATE SYMBOLS

Tree

white pine

Flower

apple blossom

Bird

robin

Fish

brook trout

Reptile

painted turtle

Stone

petoskey stone

Game Mammal

white-tailed deer

PebbleGo Next Bonus! To make a dessert using Michigan tart cherries, go to www.pebblegonext.com and search keywords:

M1 RECIPE

Gem

chlorastrolite

Wildflower

dwarf lake iris

FAST FACTS

STATEHOOD
1837

CAPITAL ☆
Lansing

LARGEST CITY •
Detroit

SIZE
56,539 square miles (146,435 square kilometers) land area (2010 U.S. Census Bureau)

POPULATION
9,895,622 (2013 U.S. Census estimate)

STATE NICKNAME
Great Lakes State

STATE MOTTO
"Si Quaeris Peninsulam Amoenam Circumspice." These Latin words mean, "If you seek a pleasant peninsula, look about you."

STATE SEAL

Michigan's state seal was approved in 1911. The bald eagle on the top of the seal stands for the United States. The eagle holds an olive branch to represent peace. It also holds three arrows to show that Michigan is ready to fight for the country. The elk on the left and the moose on the right represent Michigan. The state motto appears on the seal, "Si Quaeris Peninsulam Amoenam Circumspice." Other Latin words also appear on the seal. The word "Tuebor" in the center means "I will defend." Across the top is the Latin phrase "E Pluribus Unum," an unofficial motto of the United States that means "Out of many, one."

PebbleGo Next Bonus! To print and color your own flag, go to www.pebblegonext.com and search keywords:

MI FLAG

STATE FLAG

Michigan's flag is a field of blue with the state seal in the center. The flag once showed Michigan's first governor, Stevens T. Mason, on one side. On the other side was the state coat of arms. In 1865 the flag was changed to show the U.S. coat of arms on one side and the Michigan coat of arms on the other. The current flag was adopted in 1911. It shows only Michigan's seal. The bald eagle on the top of the seal stands for the United States. The elk on the left and the moose on the right represent Michigan.

MINING PRODUCTS

iron ore, natural gas, petroleum, portland cement

MANUFACTURED GOODS

motor vehicles and parts, fabricated metals, machinery, cereal, food processing, medicines, chemicals, paper

FARM PRODUCTS

tart cherries, sweet cherries, corn, soybeans, wheat, oats, apples, plums, peaches

PROFESSIONAL SPORTS TEAMS

Detroit Tigers (MLB)
Detroit Pistons (NBA)
Detroit Lions (NFL)
Detroit Red Wings (NHL)

PebbleGo Next Bonus! To learn the lyrics to the state song, go to www.pebblegonext.com and search keywords:

MI SONG

MICHIGAN TIMELINE

1600s French explorers and fur traders first meet the native peoples of what is now Michigan.

1620 The Pilgrims establish a colony in the New World in present-day Massachusetts.

1688 French priest Jacques Marquette starts the first European settlement in Michigan, Sault Sainte Marie.

1701 Antoine de Lamothe Cadillac builds a fort in present-day Detroit.

1751 The French have seven forts in Michigan.

1763 Great Britain wins the French and Indian wars. The British take over the French forts in Michigan.

1763 Chief Pontiac and his soldiers capture eight of 12 British forts in Michigan.

1783 When the American colonists win the Revolutionary War (1775–1783), Michigan becomes part of the U.S. Northwest Territory.

1789 The British build a fort on Mackinac Island. From there, they can control the fur trade.

1836 The Treaty of Washington takes land in both the Upper and Lower Peninsulas from the American Indians.

1837 On January 26 Michigan becomes the 26th state.

1848 The state capital moves from Detroit to Lansing because it is closer to the middle of the state.

1855 The Soo Locks at Sault Sainte Marie are completed to connect Lake Superior with the other Great Lakes. The locks allow Michigan to ship goods to more areas of the country.

1861–1865 The Union and the Confederacy fight the Civil War; Michigan soldiers fight for the Union. Abolitionists in Michigan help slaves escape to Canada on the Underground Railroad.

1899 Ransom Olds opens an automobile factory in Detroit.

1903 Henry Ford starts the Ford Motor Company on June 16.

1908 On October 1 the first Model T Ford is built; it is the first mass-produced affordable car.

1914 Henry Ford offers workers $5 a day to work in his car factories. This wage is about double the previous pay for the workers.

1936 During the Great Depression (1929–1939), autoworkers complain of poor working conditions and low pay. Workers at a Flint car factory stage a sit-down strike.

1957 On November 1 the Mackinac Bridge opens. The bridge connects the Upper and Lower Peninsulas.

1974 On August 9 Vice President Gerald R. Ford of Grand Rapids becomes the 38th president when Richard Nixon resigns.

1983 Unemployment soars because of low car sales.

2007–2009 Michigan manufacturing cities hit hard times during the Great Recession. The car industry in Michigan is especially affected.

2013 On July 18, Detroit becomes the largest U.S. city ever to file for bankruptcy.

2015 City of Hamtramck becomes the first city in the United States to elect a Muslim-majority city council.

Glossary

ancestor *(AN-sess-tur)*—a member of a person's family who lived a long time ago

ethnicity *(ETH-niss-ih-tee)*—a group of people who share the same physical features, beliefs, and backgrounds

executive *(ig-ZE-kyuh-tiv)*—the branch of government that makes sure laws are followed

industry *(IN-duh-stree)*—a business which produces a product or provides a service

legislature *(LEJ-iss-lay-chur)*—a group of elected officials who have the power to make or change laws for a country or state

peninsula *(puh-NIN-suh-luh)*—a piece of land that sticks out from a larger land mass and is almost completely surrounded by water

petroleum *(puh-TROH-lee-uhm)*—an oily liquid found below the earth's surface used to make gasoline, heating oil, and many other products

province *(PROV-uhnss)*—a district or a region of some countries; Canada is made up of provinces

region *(REE-juhn)*—a large area

resign *(ri-ZINE)*—to give up a job or position voluntarily

Read More

Ganeri, Anita. *United States of America: A Benjamin Blog and His Inquisitive Dog Guide.* Country Guides. Chicago: Heinemann Raintree, 2015.

Haney, Johannah. *Michigan.* It's My State! New York: Cavendish Square Publishing, 2017.

Yasuda, Anita. *What's Great About Michigan?* Our Great States. Minneapolis: Lerner Publications, 2015.

Internet Sites

FactHound offers a safe, fun way to find Internet sites related to this book. All of the sites on FactHound have been researched by our staff.

Here's all you do:

Visit *www.facthound.com*

Type in this code: 9781515704096

 Check out projects, games and lots more at
www.capstonekids.com

Critical Thinking Using the Common Core

1. Lansing is the capital of Michigan. What famous NBA basketball player is from Lansing? (Key Ideas and Details)

2. Mackinac Island does not allow cars. Imagine that your city or town had a "no car" rule. What would the city sound like? How would people get from place to place? Would the rule make life better or worse? Why? (Integration of Knowledge and Ideas)

3. What are the average temperatures in March for Lansing, Michigan? Use the graph on page 8 for help. (Craft and Structure)

Index